A Colt for Jenny

By Frances Bloom and Mary M. Geiger

Illustrated by Mary M. Geiger

EDUCATORS PUBLISHING SERVICE

Cambridge and Toronto

The Alphabet Series, Volume 2   Features:

Book 19	A Spotless House	initial consonant blends
Book 20	Lunch on a Raft	final consonant blends
Book 21	King Hank	ng and nk endings
Book 22	A Snake for Jane	magic e, adding -ed
Book 23	Phil the Flea	ph, ck, vowel digraphs
Book 24	The Bird Watch	r-controlled vowels er, ir, ur
		spellings for /k/—k, ck, ke
Book 25	Up in the Clouds	ow, ou, igh
		contractions: it's, let's
Book 26	Witty Word Play	consonant + le
		consonant + y endings
Book 27	A Colt for Jenny	ild, old, ind, olt, ost
Book 28	Mandy	ar, or
Book 29	The Moon Zoo	oo
Book 30	Josh, the Collector	y as a vowel
Book 31	Clancy Races	hard and soft c
Book 32	So Many Bridges	hard and soft g
Book 33	Wally Walrus	aw, au, all
Book 34	Justin's House	oi, oy
Book 35	Ella	tch
Book 36	Get Dad Lost	ing as an ending

Design: Karen Lomigora
Acquisitions/Editor: Bonnie Lass
Managing Editor: Sheila Neylon

Printed in Benton Harbor, MI, in February 2013
ISBN 978-0-8388-8752-3

9 10 11 12 13 PPG 17 16 15 14 13

Jenny was ten years old, and her
mom and dad gave her what she wanted
most—a colt!

Jenny and her mom and dad lived on a ranch. Her Uncle Danny lived on the ranch right next to them. Uncle Danny had three colts, and he sold one to Jenny's mom and dad.

Uncle Danny had picked the best colt for Jenny. It had a bright, shiny coat and looked peppy.

"This colt is not wild, but he is frisky," Uncle Danny told Jenny. "You will not be able to ride him until he is a bit older. But I will be around to help you train him."

"Wow! Thanks, Mom and Dad. Thanks, Uncle Danny," said Jenny. "I will take good care of my colt! I think his name will be Frisky."

Frisky would graze on their land most
of the time. Jenny fed him hay, too, but
just a little at a time.

Jenny got Frisky plenty to eat and drink. She kept the food and water racks clean.

Mom got Jenny a brush to help keep
Frisky's coat soft and shiny. Jenny
would brush him until she got all the
tangles out of his mane.

Jenny would check Frisky's feet. She had a pick to get the rocks and dirt out. So the colt could not kick her, Jenny would stand at his side and not behind him.

Frisky would run around the ranch.
When he would see the colts on Uncle
Danny's ranch, he would run beside them.

Frisky would chase kites and moths.
One time he ran after a butterfly!

Jenny had a lot of fun with her colt.
It was fun to see him get into things.
Frisky would eat snacks right off the
picnic table!

If their cat, Mr. Gold, was around, Frisky would poke him. Then Mr. Gold would let out a yowl and slink off.

Frisky could be sneaky, too.
Sometimes he would eat snacks right out
of Jenny's pocket!

When it was hot, Jenny would squirt
Frisky with the hose, and he would run
away. Then he would run back to play in
the mud puddles.

Uncle Danny told Jenny to first gain the trust of her colt, and then Frisky would listen to her. Jenny gave him lots of hugs and told him that he was a good colt.

When it was time to train Frisky,
Uncle Danny got Jenny a lead rope to
clip on Frisky and told her to hold the
free end tightly.

Jenny would lead Frisky around the
ring and then play tag with him. She
would tap him on his rump and then get
him to run after her.

When Frisky was too frisky, Jenny had to hold him with a firm hand. When Frisky felt a bit lazy or grumpy, Jenny had to be stern. But most of the time Frisky did his job proudly.

Jenny would say "Walk," and Frisky
would walk. When she said "Trot," he
would trot. And when she said "Stop!"
he would stop.

Jenny's dad helped her pick out a saddle for her colt. Jenny put a pad on Frisky's back. Then she put the saddle on the pad and made sure the girth was tight. Frisky did not seem to mind.

Before she could ride Frisky, Jenny
had to let him get the feel of an empty
saddle. Jenny had him walk with just the
saddle on his back. Then she leaned on
Frisky so that it would feel like someone
was in the saddle.

At last the big day came. Jenny
could now ride on her colt. She swung up
into the saddle and sat on it. Frisky did
not stir or flinch as Jenny rode him.

Jenny rode Frisky for a little while
and then got down. Mom and Dad told
Jenny that she did a good job. "Frisky
did a good job, too!" said Jenny.

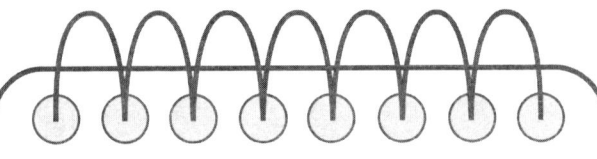

Who picked out the colt for Jenny?

What did Jenny have to do to
train her colt before she could
ride on him?

If you could pick a pet, what
would it be? How would you take
care of it?

Book 27 introduces

ild
old
ind
olt
ost

◆▼◆▼◆▼◆▼◆▼◆▼◆▼◆▼◆▼◆▼◆▼◆▼◆▼◆▼◆▼◆▼◆▼◆

Learn ▼

lived
water
walk

Review ▼

listen
their
wanted
one
someone
sometimes
so

Read ▼

The colt lived on the ranch.
He would listen when Jenny told
him to walk.
Jenny kept the water clean.
He is not wild.
It was what she wanted most.
She did not stand behind him.
He did not mind the saddle.